LIFE LESSONS

Inspiring Stories of Faith,
Family, and Friendship

MARK HOLTON

First published by That Guy's House, 2020

Copyright © Mark Holton, 2020

ISBN: 978-1-913479-51-0 (Print)

ISBN: 978-1-913479-52-7 (Ebook)

The moral rights of the author have been asserted.

That Guy's House
20-22 Wenlock Road
London
England
N1 7GU
www.thatGuysHouse.com

Introduction

I have always appreciated the love and support the Angels and my guides have given me. Through reading about my experiences and stories in this book, I hope that you can feel the same peace, love, and calmness. We all have the ability to slow down and listen to what our intuition and the Universe is saying.

Some lessons are uncomfortable and sometimes it can feel easier to avoid feeling anything. When you do feel this way, it is a perfect time to call on your Angels. Take note of how you feel when doing this. This will help you have more confidence to face the darkness.

Know that you are forever loved, held, and are a special human being in this world.

Often we are hard on ourselves, we seek perfection, and compare ourselves to others.

Three Steps To Guide You Daily

1. **Have gratitude.** Be grateful for being alive, for being able to breathe fresh air, and for having the basic necessities of life: food, water, and shelter.

2. **Create a daily affirmation for yourself.** Whatever comes natural for you. Love is my favorite affirmation as it is simple to use, and for myself has been the most challenging to face. Finding an affirmation for yourself will allow you the opportunity for growth, expansion and discovering self love, and onto divine love - the highest love possible.

3. **When you look in the mirror each day say "I love you, [your birth name].** I am loved and never alone." You will feel the love of your Guardian Angel supporting you. How you feel will follow you throughout your day. A beautiful way to see your true self in the mirror, and a great start to your day. Enjoy your journey, and thank you for being a part of my journey. Enjoy the stories and be gentle with yourself and others.

Lots of love,

Mark

Chapter 1
The PE Teacher

I arrived at the funeral home to see my dad off with a final goodbye. I was nervous, even though the day before our family was at his bedside experiencing his Ascension to Divine at Hospice House in 2008.

As I entered the room, I could feel a warmth on my shoulders as though the sun was shining down on me. In that moment, I knew my Dad (Patrick) was one of my spirit guides, and would continue to help me through my life journey. My Dad loved watching the birds every morning, and had several bird houses in the backyard. He enjoyed seeing all the commotion and excitement the birds got into at all the birdseed that was in all the houses Several humming birds would also visit, and displayed their unique ability to be still and present, then flutter away so majestically. It makes me smile knowing how happy my dad was in those moments. Even though deep down he was hurting inside. My father, not long after the summer

3

of 2006, went into long term care at age 60. But with grace and strength and so much humility that the funny memories and moments continued for another few years. I spent a lot of time visiting my dad, and helped with delivering the dinner trays and making sure my dad had two desserts if he wanted more as I often had dinner from the cafeteria, and would have extra rice pudding or green jello that was never out of supply, it seemed, at the hospital. Through these experiences I learned more about health care and the nursing team. I saw an advertisement for the Care Aide Program in Vancouver and my journey and career in health care had begun.

10 months later I moved to the Sunshine Coast, Sechelt, and started working atTotem Lodge and ShornCliffe long term care. My first job in health care.

The afternoon was warm, the sun shining in Half-moon Bay. I of course was racing to get to work. Always stuck behind the elusive one car on the highway. I know this was a good thing, a reminder to slow down, both on the road and in life in general.

I arrived at Totem Lodge rushing to hear the report, and gulping down my coffee.

The evening was going to be busy but enjoyable because I was amongst friends that felt like my second family - something I never understood until I moved to the Sunshine Coast. I began getting the residents ready for dinner. I walked into Joan's Room and I heard an excited voice saying, "Hello George how was school today?"

The other care aide in the room politely replied, "Joan this is Mark, not George."

"Tell me something George, how can you get here from school so fast? You must have Angel Wings!" Joan said. I replied, "we all have Angel Wings Joan". aww that's sweet of you to say. Joan looked up at the clock; it read 4pm. Joan replied, "it could also be that it's 4pm and school gets out at 3:15 pm. That gives you plenty of time to get to work on time."

I laughed and said, "very true Joan."

"So tell me George how do you like working with all these old broads." She asks me. The room was full of laughter.

"I enjoy it and I'm glad that I can help." I said, "Well let's get you ready for dinner Joan." I continued to get Joan ready for dinner, transferred her to her wheelchair, then we were off to the dining room. I parked Joan at her table with her other roommates, and I saw some toys, balls and balloons on the floor from activities. I turned around and cleaned up the toys, and practiced dribbling the ball like it's a basketball. I threw it into the bucket. Then from across the room I heard "George now that's not how you throw a basketball. Did you not pay attention in my gym class? We went over basketball quite thoroughly! Well after school you can practice, then you can show me what you learned at the end of the week."

Everyone in the dining room roared with laughter.

I continued to have a good shift and went home feeling happy, laughing about the evening.

I woke up early the next morning as it was Easter Sunday. I sometimes changed shifts, so I was working early that day. It was also the first Easter without my Dad; I was thinking of my family and feeling sad, but I knew that helping the residents during Easter was a good thing, and would bring me comfort. I arrived at work ready to take on the day. I started my shift and was bringing the breakfast trays into the residents rooms. I walked into Joan's room and placed her breakfast tray carefully on her bedside table. There was a beautiful Easter lily sitting in the window, large enough for everyone to enjoy. My co-worker was also in the room helping the other residents. Joan looked over at me and said, "Good morning Patrick".

I heard my co-worker explaining, "This is Mark not Patrick."

"Oh but he was just here standing by the window saying 'Hello my name is Patrick.'" Joan said.

I looked up, trying not to spill breakfast on the residents I was feeding.

"Oh my goodness", I said out loud, smiling, tears running down my cheeks. I knew what was happening. I wished everybody a Happy Easter..

"Quick look at the window!" Joan said, "there is a beautiful humming bird trying to get at my Easter Lily. He is fluttering about and tapping the window he must really want in here. George look at this."

I looked at the window crying happy tears. I saw the hummingbird and said, "Thank you so much, this is the best Easter surprise. Hello Dad, thank you, I love you."

Joan looked at me and said, "It was a beautiful Easter surprise. Oh George, there is some Kleenex on the table. Gee take the box, your eyes and nose are running, you must be allergic to my beautiful Easter Lily."

I gratefully took the Kleenex and then gave Joan a hug and said, "Happy Easter. Try to finish your breakfast. I will go get you some more coffee."

"That would be lovely." She said.

I left the room with a smile, feeling the warmth on my shoulders, like the sun shining on me. I knew it was my Dad giving me a hug and the Angels saying, "Hello son, Happy Easter."

Lessons Learned

- Know that God is forever present in our lives, all we need to do is ask for help and to call on our Angels. They will listen and give guidance and light, whenever we call on them and give them permission to guide us.

- Enjoy the work you do, and the friends and company you enjoy. Find what you are passionate about.

- Being passionate helps you to find your true calling - discovering who you are as a person and what drives you forward.

- When people are passionate their life changes. They become happier people because they have found what they love doing.

- It starts with having gratitude;stop comparing yourself to others, be grateful for what you have and start to appreciate life and all its blessings.

- The significance of being passionate opens your world to higher energy, helps towards being more creative, enjoying friendships, and exploring other hobbies or activities one has only dreamed of or talked about. It leads people to put themselves first and helps them have a better outlook on where they are now, and where they desire to go on their journey in life.

Chapter 2
Mom's Best Lasagne

Spring 1996 was an exciting time. I was in my first year of college, I had just turned 21, bought my first car, and started a new job at a video store. My first day, I started my shift, and I was introduced by our Assistant Manager Darren to Nav, Lacey, Marlee, and Corina. I learned about customer service and learned fast the layout of the store and where the videos go.

We all laughed and enjoyed each other's jokes and stories throughout the shift.

Nav asked me to come over for dinner and watch a movie, so I can meet his family and his brother. Through conversation, movie nights become a monthly event at Nav and B's house.

"Sure that would be great." I said.

"You have got to try my mom's lasagna!" Nav replied.

I arrived that Saturday for dinner at the Mann household. I was greeted by Mrs. Mann and Sandy -"You must be Mark."

I said hello and I was welcomed into the house.

The food smelled good and I'd been meeting everyone gathered in the living room. I was handed a plate and got to try this legendary lasagna I'd heard so much about.

"Save room Mark, you must try some Indian food!"

I tried the butter chicken and a few other items with curry. I took a seat in the dining room with the rest of the group of friends visiting. I started eating and immediately jumped up - it was hot, so hot!

"I need milk, milk please!" I shouted as I ran through the living room.

"There goes Mark!"

"No there goes Holts!" and there, a nickname was born. I poured a glass from the fridge as I heard laughter in the background. I started laughing and Sandy and Mr. Mann said to me, "Don't worry son, the hot curry will put hair on your chest."

I continued laughing and enjoyed the evening. I heard many stories of family, and also shared about my own family, and what I was studying in college.

The evening went by quickly. I turned and thanked Nav and his family for a fun evening of laughs and good food. I said goodnight and walked towards my car, nicknamed "The Electric Jelly Bean". It did look electric and was shaped like a jelly bean. It was shimmering in the moonlight. Before I got in my car I looked up at the sky and saw a beautiful crescent moon with very little clouds. It was bright and I could feel the cool crisp air. Autumn was on its way. I continued looking at the moon, not feeling cold but warm from the evening, and I drove home laughing to myself about the evening. I arrived home and got out of my car, still in amazement of the beautiful moon.

I looked up and continued reflecting on the evening. I realized that not only had the Mann family welcomed me into their home, they had welcomed me into their life. A tear ran down my cheek at the thought of the new friendships that had been formed that evening -friendships that I knew would be lifelong. I smiled and more tears started to flow. I wiped my tears away, looked up at the sky and said out loud, "Thank you Angels for the gift of friendship." I went inside and got ready for bed, saying my prayers.

Lessons Learned

- I learned that evening that friendships are sacred - they can help us grow as a person and can last a lifetime and beyond.

- To be open to meeting new people, be yourself and have the courage to introduce yourself in social gatherings.

- To surround yourself with people that help lift you up.

Chapter 3
Meditation with Ease

I arrived at the Mann household, and walked into the living room to see Sandy Mann with his legs propped up on the couch,lying down like he is about to do sit-ups. He turned his head,said, "Hello Mark, how's it going, how's your day? Come join me, I am meditating."

I started laughing.

"All right why not, I have never tried it before." I said.

I then propped my legs up on the couch, hoping Nav and B wouldn't walk in and see me, wondering what the heck I am doing.

"Wow," I thought, "this feels good! I can feel the stretching."

"See this is the best way to meditate. You can get all your exercising done and meditate at the same time, it's great." Sandy said.

"Yes it sure is, you can really feel the stretching. But what you are really saying is that meditating this way is better because you don't have to exercise the correct way." I replied.

"Mark, Nav and B are downstairs I think you should go join them." He said, turning towards me with a laugh.

I went downstairs and said hello to Nav and B. I was surrounded by movie posters from every genre. I looked at them with astonishment. We headed out as we were going to dinner and then a movie. I said goodbye to Sandy. He smiled and replied, "Be safe and have fun. And practice your meditation Mark, it will help you a lot."

I practice different modalities and meditation daily. It all started because of my friend Nav's father. I did not think much of it at the time but meditation and breath work has changed my life and health.

I learned that having hobbies and fitness goals are important in life. Staying active into older age will help with mental health, energy and vitality.

Sandy also taught me to try different things and venture out of my comfort zone.

The experiences I learned helped lower my blood pressure and helped with anxiety and depression. I am grateful for starting early on my journey to a healthier life.

Lessons Learned

- To learn new skills and discover what fitness routine you enjoy.

- Having a strong mindset helps in all areas of your life.

- To stay active in mind and body as much as possible.

Chapter 4
The Nursery

I had started a new job. I'd been working as a Care Aide for ten years, and I desired to see what working as service support was all about in maternity. The flowers were in full bloom, and I walked through the park daily on the way to the hospital. I would often see animals; squirrels, rabbits and ducks that would surround you if you sat on a park bench eating a chocolate chip cookie. I would often have my lunch in the memory garden. It's a beautiful flower garden with stepping stones that have the names of loved ones that families can dedicate in their memory. It was beautiful in full bloom in summer. It was a busy day at the hospital but I was doing my work and enjoying the day. Two twin girls had been born a few days previous. I went to restock the nursery and get a glimpse of them and there they were, side by side, twin A and twin B.

I admired the newborn twins as I said a blessing and welcomed in the Angels,thanking them for these two precious gifts to the world. I was humming a lullaby that I had heard the night before - the babies had called to me to listen to Praise Baby on Spotify so I did and I had the best sleep. I often get my Soul Connections through music, journaling, and the Earth Elements.

The sun was shining brightly through the window as I was praying for the twins.

"Have you noticed how bright the sun gets in the nursery lately?" I heard from the nursing station.

I smiled to myself as I knew why - it was the Angels saying hello, and

offering guidance and love. I felt the warmth as though I was standing on the beach, with the sun on my back and shoulders.

I sometimes get to see who is an indigo baby - they will have a glimmer of rainbow light just above their crown. It's a beautiful experience and reminds us how precious life is and that it's a blessing and a joy to have children and to start a family. I get the same experience by doing light work, and seeing the newborns daily.

I could also feel a presence that day. I looked up and standing next to me was Sandy Mann.

"Good afternoon Mark how are you doing?" He said to me.

"I am doing great!" I replied, "Look at these two special incredible twin girls." I smiled, looking at the newborns, "They are created with love."

I continue to feel the love and warmth around me. Sandy visits me often whenever I am rushing, getting anxious, and whenever I call on him, and of course whenever I am dancing - either on the dance floor or when I do the Ecstatic Dance.

I am grateful to know that Sandy is one of my guides. I thank him for guiding me and for his love and presence. I am pleased to know that he has Ascended to Heaven and works with Archangel Chamuel with Divine Love and Self Love energy.

My dear friend and father figure Sandy Mann left us too soon, but he is still very much a part of my life and I am blessed to have his continued love and support.

Lessons Learned

- Self love is vital for growth and happiness, and it starts with gratitude - having thanks for where we are currently on our life journey. Turn negative thoughts and self talk to more positive inner dialogue and daily affirmations - "I am loved", for example.

- To have children is a blessing from God. Enjoy starting a family, as it's a beautiful experience that I desire to have soon in my life. Don't take it for granted- yes there are days that are dark, but you have to support family and friends, husband or wife. If women are experiencing depression following the birth of a newborn, seek help, and/or talk with a friend or therapist.

- Daily meditation is not only helpful, it can change your life. It saved my life, and got me on track to creating a better life for myself.

- Meditation clears away negative energy, and improves mood, self-esteem and helps to maintain a healthy life.

Chapter 5
The Cultured Christmas Tree

I woke up early as I was excited for school; my first time ever being excited to go to school. It had been four months into grade one. That morning, I had breakfast and fought to get into the bathroom before my twin sister Melanie and older brother Mike. I found out soon after getting ready that school had been canceled for the day. My mom told me that my sister and I could do homework after playing in the snow.

I looked out the window and saw a blanket of snow, and snowbanks piled high all the way up to the rooftop of our house. There had been a record snowfall in Prince George, 1981. I quickly put on my snow pants. My jacket had a string going throughout the arms with mittens attached so I would not lose another pair of gloves. My older brother Mike would say to me, "Mom made you idiot mittens, only you would lose several pairs of gloves."

Usually I would be up early to watch Saturday cartoons, but that day my sister and I raced to get ready to play outside. We could not believe how much snow there was.

My dad let us climb the ladder to the roof as we helped shovel the snow from the rooftop. Melanie and I jumped from the roof into the snow, the snow reaching over six feet. We had so much fun as children in the winter time; we went sledding with other kids in the neighborhood, and with my friends Alison and Jason.

We were born at the same hospital in Williams Lake, and my parents became friends with the McNeils, their parents. Alison and Jason; we have been friends for almost 40 years.

Her grandpa would take us sledding on a huge hill behind our house. Melanie and I called him Gramps, and that caught on and his grandchildren continued to call Alison and Jason's grandfather Gramps. He has been a loving grandfather to many friends in the neighborhood.

We eventually went back to school and the children had built a huge snow fort. It looked like a castle made of snow, and we had snowball fights at recess and lunch. They did not last long as a child got injured, and we would be in detention if we had any further snowball fights. Winter became my favorite time of year as a child and as an adult. I loved the snow and being outside - from snow forts, to building snowmen. And I always made the biggest snow angels everywhere. It was close to the Christmas holidays, and we had finished our last day of classes before our winter break.

I had just arrived home and Melanie came soon after. We entered our living room and there was my dad and my brother Mike putting up this massive Christmas tree.

My dad said to the three of us, "This tree is called a cultured Christmas tree. Your mother wanted to try having a real tree this year and this is the best one to get as they are fuller and look better than the skinny tree we tried before."

The tree stood tall and was wrapped in several ropes as it needed to thaw out to room temperature.

Melanie and I were waiting for the tree to thaw out, wondering how long it could possibly take. After what seemed like forever the tree thawed out overnight. The next morning we finally cut the rope, and saw the tree in all of its beauty.

My dad carefully cut the string, the branches fell open and the tree was full of branches and lots of sap. It was a full tree, however the stump part of the tree did not fit the stand. So my dad had to saw part of the stump. We eventually got the tree upright and in the tree stand, but the tree was leaning to the left so my dad had to get inventive and used fishing wire through three hooks he put into the ceiling to hold the tree upright. It worked; the tree was in position, and we could begin to decorate it. I loved putting the lights on the tree; the colors were always a blur until I started wearing glasses. With them, I could see the bright colorful lights and would stare at them because they looked like twinkling stars and I could finally see them clearly. I think that's why I like Christmas lights and fireworks so much, because I remember how I felt when as a young child I could see how magical the colors were and the first time being able to see them at two years old when I had my first pair of eyeglasses.

Melanie and I carefully unwrapped our Christmas decorations - my mom had special glass ornaments from my great great grandmother. We added the lights, then the tinsel, and garlands made of popcorn. The tree looked beautiful. My mom had added several Angel ornaments, and over the years our tree became the Angel Christmas tree. With different variations of decorations from seeing the festival of trees every year; we got a lot of decorating ideas and inspiration there.

My mom called everyone into the living room,wanting our whole family to be present to see the finished tree and how it lit up the living room with the glow from the lights and decorations. We had just sat down to dinner, and started eating when, snap, snap, snap. The fishing wire had broke and the tree had come crashing down.

"Oh no, not our cultured tree!" My mom said.

You could hear a popping sound as some of the glass ornaments had shattered from the weight of the tree.

Melanie, Mike and I rushed into the living room to see the tree on the floor and broken ornaments everywhere. We didn't know if we should laugh out loud or cry. We helped clean up the mess, and my dad then had another plan to reattach the tree to the ceiling as well as adding three bricks to hold down the tree stand. There was no way this tree was going to crash down a second time.

The Christmas tree survived the holidays and we never had a real tree since, my parents buying an artificial tree the following year.

The Christmas tree incident was similar to the movie Christmas Vacation, so my brother started calling our Christmas celebrations the Griswald Holton family Christmas after our cultured tree experience.

I have fond memories of Christmas as a child, and as an adult we always celebrated amongst family and friends. After my dad died, it took myself almost five years before I started celebrating again. By that time I had moved to the Sunshine Coast, and my friend Larry and I went into the city to see all the Christmas displays throughout Vancouver.

This got me thinking about my family, and I could feel the gentle nudge of my eyes starting to get watery, as I looked at the festival of trees, and the animated Woodward's Christmas window displays. I could feel my dad's presence and I remembered the importance of family, even if we didn't always get along growing up. We always have each other to help each other through life's ups and downs.

I caught the ferry back to Sechelt from Horseshoe Bay with Larry. He mentioned how Eaton's store displays were so exciting as a child in Toronto - everything was Rudolph, as the children's story was just starting to become a tradition at that time.

I walked onto the ferry with a sense of relief and excitement; my inner child had emerged and the spirit of Christmas and the love of my family and my dad had surfaced and brought a smile to my face.

I made it home safely and woke up the next day to a surprise on my doorstep. Larry had left me a bag full of Christmas lights. I untangled them and decided to put them on my fence to add light to my driveway, as it was dark in Halfmoon Bay. I counted the strands of lights. I had 400 Christmas lights that went down the length of my driveway and lit up the yard. It certainly was a dazzling display; my neighbors called my driveway the Runway. The neighbors' children loved what I did - I could see the excitement as they were watching out of their living room window.

I had the Christmas magic back. I got a real Christmas tree on the weekend and decorated it with lights and decorations and some ornaments from when I was a child that my mom had sent to me as a reminder of Christmas from the past, and to put a smile on my face.

I learned to never forget my memories from my childhood, as we all have good and bad memories. I have learned from lots of self work to honor your inner child. The little boy inside was so thankful for celebrating and for me acknowledging him. From that day forward, I could feel my dad's presence whenever I called on him through prayer and meditation. I have learned through the study of Angels that our family's love is forever present and strong. What we can do in our own lives is take a step back to journal about your inner child and what made you happy then, and perhaps try that now in your present life.

Could be a fun activity you enjoyed that you can teach your children. Take time to be still in prayer and meditation and think about what you could bring to your current life that would help you move ahead through rough times or struggle.

When in prayer or in the stillness, call out to your loved one that has passed on as they are always with you. Always remember them and celebrate their birthday and the activities they enjoyed. Try to see how you feel and how your family feels.

Your ego will tell you not to be silly, and other negative thoughts. However your heart will tell you to do what guides you.

Journal how you feel before, during, and after this experience of remembrance. It will bring peace and happiness to you.

Cherish your memories, they help you through the bad times. Remember your family and the love you felt growing up. Not everyone has a good childhood or upbringing.

We can't choose our blood family but we can choose our friendships, relationships, and our chosen family of friends and people that care about you.

Honor yourself, honor your childhood, honor the love of family.

Lessons Learned

- The importance of embracing our inner child teaches us how to connect with creativity and play, when we are taught that it's not adult-like, or to suppress our inner child. Letting ourselves enjoy the child within helps us to be less robotic in daily life, happier and more care free.

- Family connections are important no matter what the circumstances are. Healing wounds if necessary will strengthen your soul and bring happiness as getting rid of the baggage of emotions from the past will be a huge release.

- Journaling daily can help release stagnant energy and emotions that may still be attached to us. It can be therapeutic and can turn into something that is an enjoyable activity rather than feeling like a chore.

Chapter 6
Everything Will Be Alright Child

I had started a new job in North Vancouver at a care home. It was my first summer there, and it was nice to be working in a special care Alzheimer's Dementia unit. I enjoyed the one on one and how the residents responded to me. I had left another work site as I was being bullied and dealing with harassment, and the experience had started to affect me in my normal day to day life. I did not realize that the damage had been done and it was now on a subconscious level. I started to freeze at work and in public as well, a fight or flight response our body does when feeling threatened or harmed. I had gotten used to being treated unfairly and dealing with physical and verbal abuse from the staff. I just put up with it, trying to ignore what was happening, but this is not an effective way to cope.

I thought I had dealt with my feelings and emotions, and I started counseling and also as an outpatient at the hospital. I was making progress, and I connected with the new resident who just arrived. Her name was Eva from Vancouver, but she was originally from Sweden. She began to trust me and was appreciative of all the staff that cared for her. I didn't know at the time that her insight and care would help me through a dark time, and make a huge impact in my life. I often talked about Swedish Christmas, as I experienced my first Swedish Christmas the year previous.

My mom remarried to a beautiful man named Jan, who of course was Swedish. So our family had been welcomed to new Christmas traditions that also helped revive my love of Christmas. Eva would look at me and be calm as I would stroke her head.

"Everything will be alright, it's Swedish Christmas." I would say to her. She smiled back at me and laughed every time. It brought us closer together, and I learned more about her family and the life she created for herself and her family. I also got to share about my family and all the different traditions and cultures that I did not know about but was learning.

I continued learning and growing, taking more education in hospice and end of life care from a non pharmacological and more holistic approach. It was very beneficial for me as I excelled in end of life care, it's one of many passions I have learned over the years working as a care aide. Being able to be with someone you have cared for is very special; the residents are just like family, an extension of our family. We laugh and cry together, share stories, and really connect with them as much as possible. It's been an honor and a blessing for me.

I learned more about myself through my health care journey; I learned fast that it was my calling, the Angels guided me and my dad already knew that he would be able to continue this guidance even after his death. I started to accept and listen to where I was being guided and what I was working towards. I started including my Angel work when I was helping with end of life, and this helped calm many residents.

I am very grateful to have learned many modalities in self work and self empowerment. Once I started practicing this, I had more and more visions and Angel experiences. Even more clearly since acknowledging my authentic self.

It's important to have self-acceptance - love you for being you. We often get caught up with comparing ourselves to everyone else, and take care of everyone else forgetting to take care of ourselves first. Once you do this, so many shifts start to take place, like feeling confident, and loving what you see in the mirror on a daily basis.

The inner dialogue and inner struggle stops, it's a great feeling once you change your mindset and learn to tame your ego. You can see clearly and stop any judgement of others. Once you lead with your heart, dreams start to flourish into fruition, creativity flourishes as well, and you become the person you were meant to be, not the person everyone else tells you to be.

It took me many years to understand this concept, and now it has helped me change my life in so many beautiful ways I would have never thought possible. I know that it can do the same for you in your own life. Ask yourself, what drives you? What are you passionate about?

Start taking little steps forward to your dreams and goals, and think about what is holding you back. Perhaps it's limiting beliefs that you are not good enough. Change the inner dialogue from negative to positive, even simply by saying "I love you" in the mirror.

I remember going into work and finding out that Eva was palliative and was dying, and I took the time to be with her family. Her two daughters were at her side. I called in the Angels and held Eva close to me, and her daughters asked if I would lie next to her. I gave Eva a hug with her daughter on the other side, and I could feel the love radiating back to me and her family.

It was divine love combined with her love, it was beautiful and I whispered in her ear that Angels were surrounding us. She immediately relaxed and her breathing became slower, I was stroking her hair like I often did.

"Everything will be alright," I said, "no need to be afraid, the Angels are waiting patiently for you." I kissed her forehead. "Goodbye, I love you, and so do the Angels."

Several months later, my depression and anxiety had gotten worse, I was off work for a while to recharge and to do my best to practice self care and feel normal again. I had no idea what normal was anymore. I was in a dark place having very realistic dreams and thoughts of self harm and suicide. I woke up in tears, and could remember everything that I had just dreamt about. I put on some gentle gospel music and fell back to sleep. I often put on this type of music with residents as most had been to church at some point in their lives, and I thanked my Angels for keeping me safe from harm.

I awoke early, the sun was almost rising, and I was still not fully awake. I could feel someone stroking my head. I looked up and there was Eva, stroking my hair saying, "Everything's going to be alright child."

I could feel the love, and the light was bright and clear and she looked beautiful in a flowered dress. Also with her was Sunny, a resident who loved gospel music from the south, and he was clapping his hands and singing along toSwing Low Sweet Chariot. I did not want her to see my pile of clothes on the floor. I could see the clothes and thought if I can see them I am sure she can too. She continued stroking my hair and I could feel the love from her and divine.

I awoke and started putting my hand through my hair with tears flowing down my cheek. I knew Eva was now an Angel and was helping me. I had so much calmness and peace when I woke up. This helped me during a dark time, and I learned to call on my Angels daily and thank them for the gift of life and the gift of the connections we make in life. I have gratitude daily for the Breath of Life as well as our Prana life source. Breath work is now one of my daily rituals as well as meditation, starting and ending my day with love and gratitude.

Lessons Learned

- Create daily rituals: yoga, meditation, going for a walk.

- Discover what can help you to destress, learn to not let things build up. Let your emotions and energy out.

- Have faith that everything will be alright. When we stress or try and force an outcome, it often creates more stress and the outcome will never be what we are expecting, and can lead to problems with your health.

- Visualizing the desired outcome, this helps you to focus on a more positive way of thinking and calmer energy.

Chapter 7
McDonald's Drive Thru

I had just started working the night shift at Totem Lodge. One resident in particular loved when I worked nights because I would lather them in zinc head to toe to help with her itchy skin. I did not mind and the resident,Pixie, enjoyed that even in the middle of the night I had a smile on my face. I learned a lot about her the more I worked; she used to help transport people across Hospital Cove to St. Mary's Hospital, and helped build row boats The older hospital became a hotel for a number of years in Garden Bay. She also had worked at the Hospital in many different departments. She would encourage me to not put up with any gruff, she would say, as she had noticed I would not always stand strong. I would say yes when really I meant no, and Pixie knew that I had a big heart, and would learn how to not give too much of myself, as I needed to take care of myself too.

I learned this throughout my journey in health care. Pixie told me stories of what it was like back then. Sechelt and Pender Harbour was an even smaller community and everyone knew each other. It's like that now - the community has grown but still has a small community feel to it. I loved living on the Sunshine Coast. It was a slower pace than what I was used to, but the outdoors and growing community were all important aspects in my life. It was also what I needed in my life as well.

I was seeking connections, and learning about my life purpose. I had some sorta idea of the life I desired for myself. I knew it would involve helping people, and growing in self development and spirituality.

I had settled in nicely in Half-Moon Bay, and enjoyed being surrounded by nature right down the road from me, the lakes and ocean were so clear. I knew that I would have my own place at some point, a summer home, and land with a vegetable garden. This was when I started thinking and learning about what a small, eco friendly, lifestyle meant. With the business of daily life we often forget to be grateful for the simple things:, the gift of life, a roof over our head, and clean drinking water and food.

I learned how to cook and became good at making casserole dishes that staff enjoyed at our potluck dinners.

I was glad that there was a corner store nearby with a deli. I would not have survived otherwise, being further out of town. I also learned to appreciate nature and the environment from living so close to it, and I got to experience the seasons more closely than before. I also had yard work, but I was not the greatest at it and would often need help - I had never enjoyed it as a kid growing up. I would make up any excuse to get out of it. I would have almost all the leaves raked up into piles, then my sister would throw some leaves at me and I would try to throw some back ending up with more on the ground and in my clothes than in the garbage bag.

I continued sharing more stories with Pixie. She enjoyed hearing about my childhood, and I enjoyed hearing so many wonderful stories of her life and traveling the world. Her travels to South America and Brazil she fondly remembered, and I asked her why.

"My son." She replied.

"Oh was he born there?" I asked.

"No he was conceived there on the beaches of Rio. It was glorious." She said.

"What! You're a sweet innocent granny, I don't need to know that!"

The room was full of laughter.

"Mark dear, have you not heard of the May 1st poem?" She asked.

I replied that I hadn't. She began to recite;

"Hooray Hooray its the first of May outdoor fucking starts today."

I almost dropped the lunch tray I had in my hand.

"My goodness look at Mark, his ears and face are turning red!" Pixie said, "I made him blush. See girls I still got it."

And I laughed with everyone in the room.

"Mark there is no need to be embarrassed or feel shameful around sex." Pixie said to me, "It's a gift from God, our bodies being able to be intimate with another person who we love. We are meant to enjoy life and sex."

To honor our bodies, and ourselves on an intimate level is scared. So many of us never talk about sexuality or sex because they feel uncomfortable, and we are often led to believe its wrong.

I was left thinking about our discussion as I continued my day and felt happy about the conversation and laughter of the day.

I went into work the following day, and Pixie was so excited. All this time she had spoken with such a whisper, but she had received a gift. Her speech therapist and family had purchased a headset, so that when I walked into the room, her voice was booming; there was a speaker attached and her voice was amplified.

"Good morning Mark."

I smile ear to ear and say, "It's so nice to hear your beautiful voice."

"Would you like to try my new toy?" Pixie offered.

"Sure, yes please."

I put on the headset, adjust the volume and say, "Welcome to McDonalds may I take your order?"

I looked at Pixie and she was not impressed, but we burst into laughter. I told her about my twin sister Melanie and our first job at 16 working at McDonalds. They called us the McTwins and we worked drive thru together until one day we had a disagreement and Melanie pressed the wrong button, saying some things that you would not want the public to hear. That was the last shift we worked drive thru together. I was moved to the front counter and the grill, and

I would always burn at least one batch of English muffins every morning shift.

"Mark, you're burning the muffins again! Be careful please." The morning manager would remind me.

Meanwhile Melanie still worked drive thru and checked in on me to make sure I was not upset. Melanie is good with people and protects others, and did so several times for me growing up. It's a quality we share - as twins we are connected on a deeper level.

Melanie also has a great sense of humor. One day she heard a familiar voice in the drive thru and it was our family friend from church, Susan. She wanted to play a joke on Susan, so she took her order.

"Hello Susan, it's Melanie. Sorry I can't take your order today, my dad says your evil."

There was silence across the speaker, then laughter. This became a running joke with our friend Susan. Pixie and I continued to laugh throughout the afternoon and the rest of my shift. Several weeks passed and the leaves on the trees started to change color and my backyard was vibrant colors of yellow, orange, and red. I have always enjoyed seeing the change of the seasons. Growing up in Prince George I was surrounded by the forest. I could look out my window and see the trees in the distance, a green belt of nature only ten minutes away. To be able to see nature up close and on my doorstep in Half-moon Bay reminded me of looking out the window in awe when I was a child.

I arrived at work and started my day, and brought a breakfast tray to Pixie.

"Good morning, sleeping beauty." I said.

I looked at Pixie and saw a worried look on her face. I leaned over and took her hand.

"What's wrong?" I asked.

"Mark, I think I am dying."

I tried so hard to not burst into tears, and I said, "Not today, Heaven is full. No vacancy."

Now we both looked sad, but she smiled and understood my response was trying to make her laugh. I learned that morning that the best response was to hold her hand and smile. Sitting together in silence is very powerful and can be just as effective as giving a big hug. I tell her there is nothing to be afraid of. I have always believed we live forever, I know we don't physically but I do know that we live on spiritually. We each are guided and added to the Universal divine family.

Pixie looked at me smiling, and we gave each other a morning hug.

"Enjoy your breakfast." I told her before Iwent to the washroom and burst into tears.

I already knew that she would continue to be a part of my life, and that brought me comfort as I continued on my day. Later in the week I arrived for morning shift, and found out that Pixie had passed away. I had tears and a smile as she was now surrounded with love, and in a beautiful place. I struggled with my morning, nothing was flowing or running smoothly. I was trembling a little, as I needed to let out the emotions I was feeling. It's not good to hold emotions in as they are meant to be released.

I responded to a call bell ringing in her room, but no one else was in the room as everyone was on their way to breakfast. The call bell ringing was where Pixie used to be. I went to turn it off, and feel her presence. I get Angel Bumps, the hair on my arm stands up, I say hello and hear her message to not be so hard on myself, and to be strong. I thanked her and said out loud, "I love you, speak again soon."

I felt warm the rest of the afternoon.

I learned that day to be gentle with myself and others when they speak of death. Everyone deserves to die with grace, love, respect, and dignity. I am blessed to have been able to help many people over the years, and guide families on how to do this.

Lessons Learned

- To not be fearful of death, to hold our loved ones hands and sing with them, cry with them, hug them, let them feel your presence as much as possible. Talk with them, laugh about the good memories and remember they can hear you.

- To continue to have a good relationship with your siblings. They are family and having their love and support makes a difference in your life and up to the end of life.

- To not have any regrets. Try to live each day one at a time, as they say in twelve step programs. There is no need for a bucket list, the point is to enjoy the present moments in daily life. Some people rush around life, trying to compete like they are in a race against time. Be present with oneself and with the special people in your life.

Chapter 8

Friendship Feather

We meet people in our lives that can change the trajectory of our purpose and life calling, and these friendships are called Soul Friendships. Soul brothers and sisters. Friendship that will last a lifetime and beyond into the Angelic Realm. Then there are Soulmates. I never thought they existed until I met Alex at an equity conference several years ago.

We became Soul friends instantly; he was able to see through me to my heart's centre, and knew so much about me that I had never even told him about. He too was an Earth Angel like myself. Through recent self development work, what had been coming up was about holding on and letting go. I had gotten used to holding onto relationships that didn't work, and not honoring myself by drinking heavily, having compulsive casual sex, and binge eating, or sometimes not eating at all. I felt that I was not worthy of love, a healthy relationship, or desirable. But I learned I deserved happiness, and that letting go was a good thing, whilst always remembering the people who have shaped our lives.

Learning to let things happen authentically, and not force outcomes, was extremely difficult. I had the wrong intentions around relationships - you can't duplicate someone else. This created blocks and negative energy.

I knew I had feelings for Alex from our first meeting. I knew he was someone special, especially as he taught me how to have a voice and speak up.

"You have a strong voice, and must not let anyone take your power from you. Especially you, Mark, because some people take it easily. You will grow stronger, I will show you how" Alex said on a Canada Day weekend we spent together.

He died suddenly before I had a chance to say I love you, and I was heartbroken. I knew he was my ideal partner both in alignment and energy. We could sit in silence and be comfortable, we could laugh at the little things together. I was numb for weeks after hearing the news. I again was going through a tough transition being back in the city. I was experiencing more aggressive bullying that had become physical, and I needed my friend Alex. I ended up in an emergency as I was having suicidal thoughts and idealization again, and I knew I needed help as this became a repeat occurrence. I got help and slowly there were shifts in my life...

One day, I went home exhausted from the hospital, I did some prayers and meditation, listened to soft music and drifted off to sleep. I had a dream of a man wearing white and surrounded by Angels, and a little girl handing me a feather. I awoke the next morning feeling good and realized that Alex had messaged me through my dreams that he was fine and not to be sad.

I was up early as I had a morning shift, and on my way into work I ran into Edward, an indigenous First Nations artist that worked in the neighborhood making native art. We stopped and chatted for a bit, and he said, "Mark I have something for you that will help you."

He handed me a wooden carved feather that was hand painted black, white, and red.

I froze and had tears, I knew in that moment that Alex was another friend who is one of my Angel Guides. I thanked Edward and he told me to have a wonderful day..

Alex works with ArchAngel Michael, and they both have so much love and strength, surrounded with white and blue light.

I learned how to have strength by asking, and giving permission for ArchAngel Michael and Alex for their guidance. The Angels are always there giving love and support.

We can communicate with them regardless if you can feel, see, or hear them. Through the feelings you get, you will know they are present.

I am grateful that I can still see and feel Alex close to me. Alex you will be forever a part of my life and work. Thanks for your many gifts to this world, I love you dearly.

And so it is.

Lessons Learned

- Learning to use your voice, speaking up for yourself and being an advocate for others is something that not everyone can do, but is important in the world today. Solidarity and love of the environment and people can help make good changes in work and life.

- Letting go and not holding on to so many repressive emotions is vital for optimal health and a happier outlook on life. The flight or fight response can do a lot of damage to our body when we don't release that energy. Primal screaming or having a cold shower will release the energy immediately.

- Don't be afraid of love. I have let go of the fear around love and shame. We all deserve to be loved and respected. Live life following your heart and intuition.

Chapter 9
Like A Virgin

"Hurry up Mark we are about to leave without you!" My sister said to me as I tried to put my shoes on as fast as I could. I knew my dad would never leave without me... or would he?

"Oh shit," I thought, "I don't want to find out."

I jumped into the car. My siblings and I were on our first trip to Vancouver to visit my great, great grandmother. We were all excited as our family was driving across Canada to also visit my grandparents, cousins, and family in Winnipeg.

The 1981 Mercury Zephyr yellow station wagon pulled out of the driveway and our family adventures began. I, being the smallest, was stuck in the middle seat. An eight hour drive to Vancouver was fun for a 10 year old only because my sister kept trying to get me in trouble;

"Mom, Mark punched me!"

"Oh Melanie, your brother would not do that to you." My parents laughed from the front seat. We all played car games, like eye spy with my little eye, and read Family Circus comic books, my brother played some racing games until the batteries wore out. The drive went by fast as the car went through the winding path through the Fraser Canyon, and we stopped at Hell's Gate, an AirTram that went down the canyon rock face and near the river rapids down below. I learned I was afraid of heights that day. After a fun afternoon learning about the Fraser Canyon, and how the railroad was built through the tunnels throughout the canyon, we were back on the road and made it into Vancouver in the early evening.

The hotel was close to my grandmothers and we got ready to visit and have dinner with my grandma. We arrived at a large assisted living building over 25 stories. It was surrounded by rose gardens, and many different kinds of plants lined the walkway and outdoor patio areas.

I was so excited to see my grandma, she was always happy and I loved to learn and hear about her life. She was a private woman but would share stories with the family and us grandkids when we got to know her more. We all went for dinner and my eyes were the size of saucers, I could not believe all the food my grandma got to eat. And I was allowed to have two desserts, which was a tradition that carried on when my Dad was in long term care. After dinner we were all very full, and my family made their way to the penthouse, a top level floor that had floor to ceiling windows all around looking over North Vancouver and the Wooden Roller Coaster of PlayLand.

There were several shuffleboard tables and the room was set up for bingo and a birthday party. We were celebrating my Grandma's birthday as well as all the residents that had a birthday that month. I liked shuffleboard but my sister was better at it than I was, so I did not play that long. It was time for bingo, and my brother and sister were playing more than one card. I played only one card and got bingo dabbers with bright colors. After playing a few rounds, my sister and I kept winning, and my grandma was telling everyone that together we were good luck. Many of my grandma's friends were smiling and laughing and were pleased that we kept winning. Melanie and I went back to shuffleboard when we both figured that winning more than our allowance was enough. We continued playing until it was time for cake and tea, and everyone gathered around and sang Happy Birthday. Afterwards, we all said goodbye to my grandmother, and we continued on our journey to Winnipeg.

It was a magical evening. I remember as a young child the love and laughter I felt that evening, and it has stayed with me over the years. I learned that evening that I one day wanted to care for people.

33 years later I am celebrating next month my ten years working as a care aide.

My family had a fun time at the family cabin at Gull lake, and this would be the last time as my grandparents sold the cabin a few summers later.

Five years later, I was now 15, and our family was making the same trip to Winnipeg, only this time we were starting in Kamloops B.C. Stopping to visit our family friends the Thornly family.

Our families would spend many Easters together growing up, and many weekends camping at Shuswap lake. We spent a few days with the Thornly's and our last night our family stayed at a hotel as it was a busy time since we were at a wedding.

After a relaxing swim and a dip in the hot tub, I went back to the hotel room already in my pajamas, and started flipping the channels on tv and there on HBO was the Madonna

Blonde Ambition Concert from Barcelona. I was glued to the television.

My dad kept pretending to read the newspaper, but finally he put the paper down and watched the concert, glancing over at mom who was unsure what would happen next, but continued watching as she was out voted on what to watch on T.V.

Like A Virgin was playing and I wanted to get up and dance. I loved the music, and I knew I had to see the Queen Of Pop live at some point.

I was still excited from watching the concert, but I eventually fell asleep. Early the next morning my dad drove 13 hours from Kamloops to Moose Jaw Saskatchewan, where he kept us all awake by cranking the music. My dad had upgraded the station wagon, which was gifted to my brother Mike, and now we had the air conditioned comfort of a 1990 Astro Mini-Van with a booming stereo system. We journeyed on with Janet Jackson Rhythm Nation cassette tape on repeat, the song Escapade cranked up, and Kim Mitchell singing about Patio Lanterns would soon follow. We only stopped when necessary and that would be for a washroom break and to stretch our legs. On one occasion my mom ran towards a corn field; we were now in a different province, Saskatchewan corn on one side of the highway and wheat on the other. My mom had gone into a corn field and took some corn, coming back to the minivan with her arms full.

"Kids, don't ever do what I just did."She said.

We all laughed but being on someone's property puts yourself in a dangerous position, and we all learned a valuable lesson while also having fresh corn that evening. We thanked the farmer and the land. Finally we made it into the city of Moose Jaw and settled into a hotel and soon went to bed. We all were exhausted, especially my dad as he did most of the driving.

The next day we were only four or five hours from Winnipeg, and the excitement was growing as we finally drove into the very busy city of Winnipeg. My dad pulled into the driveway of my aunt and uncle's home - Larry and Denise., We had made it, woohoo, and our family had an enjoyable holiday that summer of 1992. From going to a Blue Bombers football game, to the Red River exhibition and being terrified from going into the wrong haunted house thanks to my uncle Larry. Having many BBQ's and relaxing by the pool. We got to reconnect with family, cousins, and our grandparents. It was a long trip but reconnecting with family helped me through my teenage years, as I was a very shy quiet child.

The time had come for us to journey back home to Prince George. I slept most of the time and after two days of driving, we made it back home. We all fought for the shower and bathroom, after which getting changed into our pajamas and heading off to bed.

It felt nice to be home in my own bed, and I awoke to the sunshine pouring through my window. I was surprisingly up early. It was near the end of August so school was a few weeks away from starting, and I was going into grade 9.

Later that afternoon my friend Rick came over and we were playing lawn darts and croquet in the backyard, then we went inside to have lemonade and to cool off.

I put on a Madonna CD, and went into the kitchen to get lemonade and cookies.

I walked into the living room and Like A Virgin is playing loudly on the stereo and my friend Rick had two small cushions from the couch stuffed under his shirt.

"I made it through the wilderness! Like a virgin, touched for the very first time." Rick was singing at the top of his lungs.

My ears and face went red. I almost dropped the tray of cookies and lemonade. I yelled out to wait, and I ran back into the kitchen and went through my mom's baking and

Tupperware drawer to find two medium sized baking funnels. I stuffed them under my shirt and ran back into the living room, both of us laughing and singing the rest of the song as loud as we could. I was hoping my parents would not walk in the front door. The laughter continued. I

"You must have seen the concert." I said to Rick.

"Yes it was on Much Music, that's how I learned all the lyrics." He said.

We both finished the lemonade and cookies, and Rick made his way home.

That afternoon I knew I had feelings for men. It didn't feel strange but my fears at the possibility of being gay stayed with me throughout my teenage years and into my late twenty's.

I came out as a gay man at 26 and for several years following learned to love myself for being me, no matter what. I started developing my spirituality, and listening to what my intuition and Guardian Angel were saying and just started really listening and following the guidance that had been shown to me. The love of my family, close friends and my Angelic team helped me during the struggles of growing up, and in daily life. I realized that we really are never alone, and to break through the fear that holds us back takes daily practice. We all are on the journey of life, different stages but all of us have love and light from within.

Lessons Learned

- Make time for friendships. We all say at times that we are too busy.

- Be proud of who you are. We all are born with love and light from the divine.

- Have laughter in your life. Laughter is a good stress release and has a calming effect on our body.

Chapter 10

Cheeseburger Cheeseburger Cheeseburger

I had started grade nine and was finding it difficult trying to fit in - I had a good group of friends but was feeling unsure of who I was. I was a band geek, and had taken music lessons since grade five. This brought me lots of confidence and helped me to not be so shy, and the concerts and music festivals helped me through grade school.

During this time I met my friend Stamatis who was also in band, and we both had the same group of friends. Nintendo was getting more popular, and our group of friends always exchanged video games; I was getting good at Super Mario Bros 2. I learned how to wrap, or beat, the game thanks to Stamat. The video games and our camping trips as a large group of friends in the summers through high school brought our friendships closer, and going to smaller high school was great because everyone got to know each other growing up.

Our camping trips were fun, and we often got chased by the Forest Rangers for setting off fireworks on the beach. This was not great for my parents as the last name Holton was banned at several campgrounds that summer.

Over my high school years our group of friends would go and eat at Mr. Jakes. My friend Stamat and his family ran a Greek restaurant and there we would always be welcomed by Stamat's family. Rob, Seneca and I would often tease Stamat's dad by speaking into the microphone, "Cheeseburger, cheeseburger, cheeseburger", laughing loudly in reference to the SNL Saturday Night Live skit about a Greek restaurant. Like the T.V. skit your number was called out over the microphone to pick up your order.

This always brought laughter, throughout the restaurant and the kitchen and Alex, Mr. Maritsas, always knew who it was. I would often hear, "Careful Marko, you might have to eat all three cheeseburgers one day."

Growing up I was blessed to have good friendships that have carried over into lifelong friendships. I learned so much about having laughter and a sense of purpose in your life and to do what you are passionate about. I heard that a lot growing up but looking back at all my experiences it's something that always got through to me. I worked many different career paths that challenged me creatively and got me out of my shell.

I also have been blessed to be from a small town: Prince George. You get to know people and be part of the community, a lot easier than you would in a larger city. This also included getting to know my friend's families and being introduced to Stamat's grandparents. A joyful grandmother and grandfather who gave me several Greek coins and told me all about Greece, and that I should travel there one day.

Before long we were all nearing grade 12 and graduation, and planning on going different paths.

I started in college that fall, and did not do well at all. I was failing some classes, and had lost my creativity and drive. I was not following my passions, and it showed.

I made the move to Vancouver and went to film school the following year; this was more of what I enjoyed and I worked in and out of the industry for several years.

Still something was missing and I could not figure it out. I ran away with Cirque Du Soleil later that year, and my new job took me to Australia. I then had to face my fears head on. I was very co-dependent at that time and had very low self esteem. It was taking the job with the circus that opened my eyes to creativity in its many forms. I worked through being more independent. Walking along the seawall at Bondi Beach it hit me that I have lots to offer, and have a great skill set. I was always living in fear, and knew I could pursue many things but how? I learned more about myself through my many walks on that seawall. I heard the call to follow my heart and dreams so I started to take action. I ventured back to Prince George, and being with my family was important for me and helped me pursue my purpose and calling.

My dad was soon living in long term care; this opened my eyes to the health care team, and later in the year I moved back to Vancouver and went back to school in the care aide program. The program challenged me in ways I never thought was possible; we were learning about end of life care while I was learning and experiencing first hand with my father in hospice.

I wanted to give up and stop everything, but I had the strength of my classmates, family and friends that helped me to go forward with my studies. I then really started meditation and exploring what sacred space was for; it added to my comfort and opportunities started to flourish. I moved to Sunshine Coast as I mentioned in earlier chapters and started my journey of self discovery, health care, and found myself, my purpose and what I am here on this earth for.

I had beautiful experiences with the divine, and it started to be a daily ritual to speak to my blood family and my Angelic family. It's a wonderful feeling knowing that we can talk to anyone we desire, living or passed on, just by getting quiet and calming our thoughts and nerves, meditation, breath work. It connects us to higher energy to be able to do this.

I also had more darkness resurface that I tried hard to ignore. It is helpful to clear your mindset by getting back to what makes you feel good, or what can happen is an endless cycle of self sabotage, shame and guilt. I had been in the workforce for five years and was back in the city, and I thought one way to drown out my emotions was to drink and find love in the wrong places. I learned fast that I cannot find love especially if I had no respect for myself and my body. That energy came back in situations and people that I met but never gave me respect, treating me like garbage. That's how I felt inside so I thought it didn't matter if people treated me badly. We all deserve to be loved, and that's what God teaches us - to love ourselves in all our beauty, and to not feel ashamed. It's normal and healthy to be sexual but not when you purposely put yourself in harm's way. That is not a healthy way to deal with problems and emotions.

71

It was an intense time for me, I just could not get out of the darkness. I refused to do any spiritual work, or take care of myself emotionally and physically. I was at my breaking point,lost it, and was crying and yelling out in my bedroom, why?

I wanted to end the suffering and the cycle of feeling so numb and helpless.

As I continued to cry out and collapsed on my bed, I was able to calm down and catch my breath. I was getting frustrated as I reached out and no one was available. I called the help line and they helped me calm my nerves. I got comfortable on my bed, but I was still upset and shaken. I was thinking that I might need to go into treatment for alcohol and sex addiction. Or at least to better manage compulsive behavior.

I then heard a voice;

"No you don't need to Mark. We are here to guide you and support you."

I was having a vision of my friend's dad Alex, Mr. Maritsas. He had suddenly passed away a few months previous. He was standing there on the beach, surrounded by family.

The grandparents I met through Stamat's family surrounded me as well.

Grandma handed me a Greek coin just like the one I had on my altar.

"Take this coin Mark," She said, "it will give you comfort and safety when you travel. Come join us in Greece, you must try not to live in fear. You are being loved, and held by all of us."

I cried happy tears and could hear the waves, and feel the hot sun. "You got this Marko, don't feel bad about yourself. You are loved and there is never any judgment. Enjoy life and your family and friends. Call on me whenever you feel down, or need support."

There were several Angels all around me, including the Maritsas family. I felt so much love and the sunshine was out the whole time, and I drifted to sleep until I awoke the next morning.

I did not feel like harming myself, or any anger or darkness, after this experience. I knew that I just had to ask for help whenever I needed support and guidance.

I rarely go to a dark place but sometimes your Ego and inner voice can be very persuasive and they will resurface unexpectedly just to keep us on our toes. What we can do is ask for help from our Angels, Buddha, whoever we feel connected to. Call a helpline when in distress, or a friend or family member. We always have support and guidance, we are fully supported in this lifetime and beyond. May you feel the love and light on a daily basis.

And so it is.

Lessons Learned

- Believe In yourself, and know that we all have different strengths and skills to shine.

- Be proud of who you are - we all are born with love and light within us.

- Have laughter in your life. Having a good laugh is a healthy stress release.

Chapter 11

Angels And Spirit Animals

Some of my fondest memories from childhood are from Christmas holidays.

From jumping off the roof at 5 years old because the snow was so deep it was piled right up to the roof to building snowmen, and my favorite,snow angels. I made them everywhere, even in Half-moon Bay under the Milky Way and stars on a cold winter's night.

I first had my soul connection to Divine at Christmas time. I would look at things funny; I loved the colors of the lights, and until I was 2 years old was cross eyed so saw double of everything - no wonder I made funny faces. But when I did get glasses and I could see properly, what did not change was the Angel colors I still continued to see and the Auras around the people that I saw and cared about. The blue, pink, yellow, green, white, and red silhouettes that would stand out. I did not know until many years later what they represented or the meaning behind this beautiful light.

The colors and Auras are the warming light that Angels are surrounded with; everyone has a different color, humans and Angelic beings. We all emit light whether we want to or not, it is part of our birthright as we are born with a Guardian Angel right through our life cycle to the end of life.

I would have different experiences that made my day - I would be thinking of someone and then they would call me moments later, a synchronicity that was the universe sending me little reminders to be gentle with myself, and my thoughts and emotions. I often felt like I was walking uphill carrying this massive boulder, and then having to push the boulder up the steep slope. Only to run down the other side to get out of the way from getting run over or squashed by it. It was meant to be gentle, reminding me not to make things more difficult for myself. Let things be, stop trying to control the outcome.

Angels are part of my daily life; they always show up, and will be sending messages by dropping feathers, or number sequences non stop sometimes to get my attention. My connection is music, meditation, and journaling. What are your ways of connecting to source? Having a daily routine for reflection helps us move through the work week with ease and through life without any sudden boulders chasing us down. It helps us to grow spiritually and before you know it we have the skills to take on anything that comes our way-without going into self sabotage and letting our comfort zone take over.

Angels also send us love and blessings through the animals in our lives. Whether you have a pet here on earth or a pet who has moved on to heaven, their loving blessings surround us. Our connection to the animal kingdom brings joy and peace in our lives. Our beloved pets are an extension of the family; celebrate their birthday and keep these memories alive. People get assigned a Spirit Animal, and they are very similar to our Guardian Angel - the spirit animal guides us towards inner strength, environment and the qualities in the animal are magnified through the person. In their quality of character and personality, how we treat others.

Animals also have souls like humans, and feelings and emotions, so they too have the gift to return home to heaven. Many cultures believe in Spirit Animals and their significance to humans, the land and energy. Our connection to nature is magnified when we incorporate the animal kingdom into our lives - we take better care of Mother Earth and the animals that live on the land, and also take better care of each other.

Lessons Learned

- To acknowledge the land and earth with respect - nourish the earth and it will nourish you.

- Love and learn from animals. They are insightful and can bring comfort and teachings to us when we least expect it.

- Listen to what the Universe is saying to you - Angel numbers or feathers, the beautiful Angels are getting your attention for a reason.

Chapter 12
Irish Jig

I had started caring for an Irish lady at work, and I got to spend more time with her as I was working full time as a care aide. I have Irish roots in my family, so I was naturally interested in learning more about Ireland 's magical beauty and earth elementals, fairies, and flowers, and the folklore made sense to me. I have been called to this magical place, through my dreams and visions. I look forward to one day discovering Ireland's beauty in person.

I was having a tough time. It was in the middle of winter and I have always struggled with seasonal mood changes; depression and anxiety added to the mix made for a long winter time ahead. Working night shifts helped me to avoid my emotions and how I was really feeling. It led to a downward spiral of feeling lost, disconnected, and numb with no emotions at all. Was I still alive? How could this be happening when I had always been happy and motivated? These were questions that ran through my mind daily. I would be on my way to work and would be ready to cross the street and suddenly would feel like I was stuck in quicksand, sinking fast.

I learned that this was a response to trauma I had experienced, but it was embarrassing as it was often followed by a panic episode where I would become the deer in the headlights and not be able to move. Fight or flight response became a normal emotion for me, and had started to affect my health as it is stressful on the body. As a way of coping I started cycling to work; I would ride my bike, rain or shine, daily. It felt good, and I continued throughout the winter, then carried on into spring and summer. I also learned how to optimize my health. What I was eating made a huge difference - I cut down on sugar, and had a better balanced diet. I was becoming a whole person again. Art therapy and expressing my inner child helped me to get creative and laugh at the little things again.

I took a leave from work to do some self care. I started the journey of getting help, facing my fears and asking for help. I soon learned better coping skills and let go of the fear of judgment. I remember having a breakthrough session in therapy, and walking out of the Mental Health and Addictions Centre as an outpatient happy, but then ran into a former co-worker and the look on their face said it all. For a few seconds the feeling of shame came over me, then anger, then happiness. I said hello and we talked for a short time, and I had no shame in talking about myself. A huge breakthrough stopped the negative self talk and turned the negative into positive ways of dealing with my inner conflicts. Even if that meant tearing apart a couch cushion, I was in a safe place to get the anger and hurt emotions out.

People don't like to face vulnerability and talk about what's really going on, it's easier to sugarcoat things and ignore. It never works though and that's how people like myself got on the merry-go-round of loving myself then self destructing. Our inner critic can bring out our worst, and it feels good to feel it and sit with the emotions. Then the comeback to simplicity and happiness is not as difficult as it needs to be.

After three years of therapy and inner work, I was able to face autumn and winter with minimal conflict. I still had a deer in the headlights response in certain situations but was able to talk myself through everything. I called on my Angels more and more for support and guidance and they sure listened. By showing me a glimpse of what my future could be like - I kept having mini visions, I called them, like taking a quick holiday somewhere pleasant and warm. Download Central became a normal daily occurrence so I started journaling and writing what was happening. I talked with other friends who are lightworkers and they all had similar experiences. I started to see other people that I knew in the visions. So my journal for once was getting filled with ideas, solutions, and experiences. My guidance into Angelology and lightwork had begun. I accepted the call for my life purpose and soul calling.

So much resurfaced, similar feelings to when I came out as gay. Now I was coming out again as my full authentic self as a lightworker and intuitive person. Once I said yes to the call, I was visited almost daily by friends, family and the angelic team from above, mostly by what music I was playing. I started playing the same music at work to calm the residents and it also calmed me when trying to fall asleep.

I was almost asleep early one morning at 4 am and a Irish song was playing from a calming playlist I created. I saw and heard from across the room, "Oh lovey, I hope you will get up out of bed and dance an Irish Jig with me. I am here to teach you Mark. Come on now the sun is rising soon let's dance."

Now wide eyed I got up out of bed with my headphones on and danced around my room with Tess, the Irish woman I'd cared for months earlier. It was fun and healing at the same time, all my fears lifted away, and I felt so calm and energized. I continued dancing and fell back onto my bed, where I saw and felt giant wings embracing me and reminding me I was loved and held.

I also learned that if I need to have a good night's sleep, I can let my guides know that I love and appreciate them, but need a good night's sleep as well. A balance that I am learning as many like to visit at nighttime. I loved seeing Tess surrounded by green light. She works with Archangel Raphael whose name means 'God heals'. He is the doctor of God and is surrounded with his emerald aura and light. Archangel Raphael helps us to heal, and guides us on how to heal ourselves. When we have a clear positive mindset, and a healthy outlook, our body and the Universe respond with joy.

Lessons Learned

- Be able to face your fears, and sit with the emotions no matter how uncomfortable it is.

- Dance, sing, move your body. It lifts our spirits and clears any negative energy.

- Be proud of yourself, we all are unique in many different ways

Chapter 13

Chocolate Chip Soul Cookies

The daily visits continued.

"Angels and friends welcome", I would say when they were in the same room, or at the beach by the ocean. It's the clearest channel for myself and the strongest energy that I find is water and the beach. My therapy continued from angry little Mark who would scribble outside the lines and make angry pictures, to calming and beautiful pictures of sunsets and sunrises, and of course hummingbirds.

Yet I somehow got on the merry-go-round again and let my ego get in the way. Sometimes it can disguise itself and be like a trickster and take control over months, and kaboom you have a moment of realization that you have not been listening to the right voice. Sometimes it takes a major shake-up to realize what is happening and mostly when we fall back into our comfort zone because it's safe, and controlled.

Well things got dark fast and nothing was going right. I stopped all the good things that I had been working on, I had a very angry and negative outlook, and the emptiness, lack ofself worth and shame resurfaced. I kept feeding the emptiness, with comfort eating, sex and alcohol that definitely didn't fill the void. Well, my Guardian Angel was trying to get my attention and called on my dear Swedish friend Eva for extra support. I was feeling the love and the message they both gave me; that I am worthy of love, happiness, and greatness. I surrendered all the negative feelings, and let my Guardian Angel take all the darkness and low energy from me, allowing it to deflect and disappear to the Universe.

I got back into journaling and writing again, but was having nightmares so my sleep was all over the place. I would sleep for a few hours, wake up, sleep some more. What scared me was the content of the dreams, as they were very dark and violent. I did more energy clearing, and protection. This helped, and I learned to clear the energy before protecting oneself, else the negative energy can stay attached to you.

I fell asleep after some meditation and calming music, and was visited by my friend Nicholas' grandmother. Nicholas is a friend and has coached me on mindset and entrepreneurship. There at my bedside was my friend's grandmother with an apron on over her floral dress. She was carrying a plate of chocolate chip cookies and my bedroom filled with the smell of them.

"I am sorry dear but these cookies are not for you." She said, "They are for our tea party, I just finished baking them."

We both laughed as my first question was how would I eat them.

"I am here to help you, Mark, you are a student of my grandson. Let's get to work."

I had some blocks in my journaling and writing and was being guided to work through the blocks and trust myself and the Angels. I had a message to give to my friend Nicholas as well - we both were experiencing blocks and frustration in our entrepreneurship goals. Nicholas had done a blog and a YouTube post while making chocolate chip pancakes.

"There were so many chocolate chips Mark," His grandmother said to me. We laughed and smiled. "I am so happy that my grandson is enjoying coaching people, and will get through this just like you Mark. When I am finished here pick up the notebook and pen and start writing again. Also tell Nicholas to keep making chocolate chip pancakes and cookies. We need to name the cookie recipe that you can pass on to him. Let's call them chocolate chip Soul cookies, made with love from your heart and kindness. Keep going forward, Mark, with love and kindness. I am so happy to meet you, call on me whenever you need help or want more baking advice."

I woke up to the sunrise and had a major craving for chocolate chip Soul cookies.

Lessons Learned

- To believe in yourself. When things are difficult, know that you will get through, becoming a stronger person.

- Try new things like baking or art. Have hobbies that you enjoy and challenge you. They help you to build the skills and confidence to be able to problem solve through life's ups and downs.

- Appreciate your grandparents, we all learn so much from our family that has lived through so much in their lifetime. They have stories to tell and wisdom to teach.

Acknowledgements

Eleven years ago, I was sitting on the beach at Sargent's Bay with my friend Larry and was telling him a story about one of the residents I cared for. We both were laughing, and he enjoyed the story I told him. He mentioned I should write a book of the stories and experiences I have had in health care. Well, a light bulb went off, and my journey in writing started.

Thanks Larry, for your friendship, love, and support. What a journey it has been; laughter, tears, and a walk down memory lane. Thank you also for believing in my dream and encouraging me to make it happen.

Thanks to That Guy's House and Sean Patrick for this incredible opportunity.

The team at That Guy's House have been like my second family.

George Lizos my mentor, friend, and writing coach. Thank you for guiding my vision forward.

My family, Melanie Orlando and Dave Orlando. Thank you for being in my life, I love you, and thanks for teaching me how to be my own protector. Thanks Dave, for keeping my twin sister safe, loved, and supported.

Mike Holton, I love you and I am thankful for the laughter and memories growing up. Melanie and I always tried our best to get you in trouble.

Michelle, thank you for being a part of our family, and for being in my brothers life.

Jan and Carol Ullstrom. Mom, thank you for your love and support, and for always helping me reach for the stars, and encouraging me to follow my heart. Jan and the Ullstrom family, thanks for your love, encouragement and for welcoming us into the family.

Josh Holton and Brenda, thanks for your love and showing me how important strength and ambition are in life.

Dr. Nav Mann and family. Thank you for your friendship and including me as part of the family – this has helped me grow as a person and has been life changing.

Stamatis Maritsas and family. The laughter and stories from our friendship, and your Dad's presence in the community, will always be remembered. Thanks for our friendship.

The Three Santa Bears Columbine, Frolic, Merlin. Thank you for your friendship, love, and support. Living at The House of Four Wands has been life changing for me.

The Mills Family and my grandparents Art and Evelyn Mills, thanks for helping me spread my Angel wings.

My grandparents Mrytle and Bernie Holton and family. Thanks for all the memories and love. My childhood was fun and exciting, and I will never forget the many summers we spent at the cabin.

William and Edith, thanks for your friendship; your stories and tea parties inspired me to write my own stories for the world.

Myles Verigin and Ericka Rankin Friesen, thanks for your friendship, and for being on this journey with me.

Spencer Raymond Madden and Jenna Faye Madden thanks for your coaching, friendship, and for showing me how to dig deep when working through emotions and experiences.

Jared Grantham and Abergale Bremner, thanks for seeing me and coaching me how to have limitless love and confidence in my life.

Thanks to Nicholas Dodge for your friendship, and for coaching me on entrepreneurship and challenging me to work towards my goals.

To all my friends and family, thank you for your love and support on this journey.

Thanks to Seryna Myers. Your shining light, laughter and friendship has helped me on this journey.

To my Soul Family, thanks for helping me rise up, awaken, and see life's many opportunities and adventures.

Lots of Love,

Mark

Afterword

Thank you for reading my journey. The Universe and Angels are always in support of you. May you enjoy your journey, remembering to laugh, love, and shine brighter each day.

Author Bio

Mark Holton is a certified Angel Guide, with a mastery in Angel card reading by Kyle Gray's Angel Team. Working with Angels, the earth elements, and Elementals has empowered Mark as a skillful and insightful light worker. When Mark is not doing energy work, he can be found swimming in the ocean with the mermaids, doing Spirit Animal Meditations, and journaling in nature. For more information, go to @mark_holton_

CPSIA information can be obtained
at www.ICGtesting.com
Printed in the USA
BVHW031533271021
619971BV00007B/250

9 781913 479534